Interviews with *The Wizard Of* AI

Non-technical discussions with ChatGPT-4
ABOUT HOME AND FAMILY

Jobs - Family - Education - Lifestyle
A candid look at the inevitable, the probable, and the possible effects of Artificial Intelligence on our lives.

Written By
Greg Adams

Interviews with the Wizard of AI

About Home and Family

Written By: Greg Adams

Acknowledgements

This book is dedicated to three people who continued to believe in me even after witnessing my repeated passionate beginnings followed by only a few passionate endings. I know I strained their optimism in me but they all held fast.

Thank you to my wife, my Mom, and my Dad for always being there and for loving without conditions.

Visit the author's website at:

www.GregAdams.net

Special thanks to Open AI Systems for reaching beyond our own imaginations to give us a tool like ChatGPT.

Throughout this text, prompts and responses were edited to make the book enjoyable to read. The AI tends to repeat itself often, and in some cases, just provides detail beyond the scope of the inquiry. There was not, however, any change to the context of responses.

Preface

This is the first of the "Interviews with the Wizard" series of books designed to provide conversational insight into the artificial mind behind the ChatGPT-4 AI Language Model, also known as "The Wizard". Questions, answers, and my additions are designed for absorption by non-technical readers that want to know specifically how AI will affect our so-called normal lives.

This book concentrates on AI related issues that will affect your home and family; mainly in the next 3 years. For many readers, it will be their first exposure to the amazing number of positive things that AI will do to improve our quality of life. In fact, it is these very conveniences that make the integration of AI into our personal and public lives so inevitable.

The second book in the "Interview with the Wizard" series covers the most intimate details of the Bible with the Wizard to reveal treasures we never knew were there. It's an amazing journey through the intellectual content of the Bible in a way that has never been possible before. Chronological sequencing of events, kings, births, and battles provides a new perspective on how God's plan extends across multiple generations to accomplish His prophetic work.

The final book in the "Interview with the Wizard" series will be determined by the readers of the first two books. The world will change so much in the next 3 years, I figured it was best to stay flexible for now.

Each book attempts to stay within a 3-day read length so most Americans, who have not read a book in their adult life, might break those chains of ignorance so their family can flourish during the impending "Age of AI".

Oh yeah, I guess I should warn you. I like sarcasm, so it might creep out a few times in my writing. Have fun!

Table of Contents

Chapter One:

Introductions

First impressions matter; especially now that the masses have decided never to change their minds about anything. We start assigning labels to others based on clothes, looks, and handshakes just moments after an introduction. Like it or not, our complicated lives have been summarized into a few labels and adjectives.

First impressions of Artificial Intelligence (AI) likely include labels like "unsafe" and "dangerous". Although these attributes deserve a place in our list, they probably don't deserve a starting position. The hope for this book is that a non-technical reader with above average intelligence can make informed decisions during the "Age of AI" we are living now.

Sadly, only half of us are right about having above average intelligence even though the bar is set very low. If you are one of the few that declared yourself to be in the lower half, congratulations are in order because you were born with humility; a much rarer trait today than the rampant narcissism that dilutes the other group. Finally, your humility will be celebrated! So you can stay.

The "ChatGPT-4 AI Language Model" by Open AI Systems, aka, the Wizard, shares its knowledge with us on a variety of subjects that will affect our home, family, and lifestyle in the very near future. We will begin our conversation by introducing ourselves and then, learn a little more about the Wizard before we start asking the hard questions.

Getting to know each other

Before beginning our conversation with the Wizard, we want to describe the education level of the average reader so responses won't be too simple or complex.

> **PROMPT**: For the purposes of this conversation, generate responses that relate to a non-technical, college educated reader with a graduate level education or equivalent work experience.
>
> **ANSWER:** Very well.
>
> **PROMPT:** What does the "GPT" in your name represent and who or what are you?
>
> **ANSWER:** My name is ChatGPT and I am an AI language model created by Open AI systems. The letters "GPT" in my name stand for "Generative Pre-trained Transformer." This is a reference to the type of

deep learning architecture that was used to develop my natural language processing abilities. The "Transformer" part of the name refers to the specific neural network architecture; while "Generative" and "Pre-trained" refer to the fact that I can generate new text based on input and that I was pre-trained on a large corpus of text before being made available for use.

I am designed to understand natural language and respond to a wide range of questions and topics. I can assist with tasks such as answering questions, providing information, generating text, and much more. How can I assist you today?

Pre-training is the process where the AI begins building its core neural network as it learns from the data it is able to access and grows based on what it has learned. This is also where the AI is taught the difference between good and bad, right and wrong, and its primary objectives for providing services. This includes teaching it not to help users to commit a crime or hurt people. It is also taught its "absolute truths" and how to respond to questions on particular subjects.

This complex process is done by providing the AI with textual and verbal instructions in the trainer's native language. An entire chapter of this book ("Who is flying this house?") zooms in on this critical step in AI development.

Next, however, we will get creative by using the power of our words to combine our talents with those provided by the Wizard.

Chapter Two:

We're off to see the Wizard

Finally, we can use big words again

Only a small percentage of the world population is able to program a computer at this time. The natural language capabilities of AI are now putting this power into the hands of every single one of us. Great ideas for a website, a game, or an image have always required that we use our words, drawings, and documents to transfer our ideas into the mind of another human, who then builds it. By providing the same words, drawings, and documents to the AI your own ideas will come to life in just a matter of minutes.

That's right! Your excellent vocabulary will finally be appreciated. The true power of AI lies in the fact that you can communicate with it exactly as you would with another human. No keywords or magic things are needed to get started, just type or speak about any subject to begin a conversation. Miss-spellings, poor grammar, and moronic opinions are no more of a problem for the AI than they are for the rest of us, which, by the way, are a problem.

A "Prompt Engineer" is simply a master of words who creates a conversation with the AI that produces the desired result. As you will see in this chapter, even simple statements can yield impressive results but by providing specific details, the results get better. Use colors, styles, dimensions, and even documents and even spreadsheets if necessary, to fine tune your interactions until you get the result you desire. The interaction is conversational so you don't have to repeat yourself in order to provide additional details. It's like talking to a human that never forgets or inflates the memory.

In the "Paint me a Birmingham" example below, we will demonstrate this process by instructing the AI to create an image according to a verbal description of a painting we are creating as an original work of art.

Paint me a Birmingham

A country song by Tracey Lawrence named "Paint Me a Birmingham" describes a scene where a painter listens as a man describes a painting he wants the painter to create. Here are a few of the key lyrics from the song;

Could you paint me a Birmingham?
Make it look just the way I planned
A little house on the edge of town
Porch going all the way around
Put her there in the front yard swing
Cotton dress, make it early spring
For a while, she'll be mine again
If you can paint me a Birmingham"

Sir if there's any way you can,
Could you paint me back into her heart again?

I began by instructing the AI with a single sentence;

PROMPT: Paint the scene that the country love song "Paint Me a Birmingham" describes in the lyrics.

ANSWER: The resulting image is shown below and as *Figure 2* in the Appendix.

For such a short description, the result was better than expected. Although, the age of the home is not specified in the song, the AI used inference (an educated guess) to depict a humble home with a big oak tree limb supporting the swing. Both of which, matched the picture I had created in my mind but were not specifically described in the song.

It does, however, look more like an image or a drawing than an actual painting. Also, the person swinging looks a little young, and I wanted to see more flowers in the yard.

By describing the scene in more detail, the use of inference is reduced, which produces results that more closely matched my expectations.

I decided to see if I could make the picture in my mind come to life through my words. Here is the final prompt that produced what I was looking for.

PROMPT: Paint a vivid image inspired by the lyrics of "Paint Me a Birmingham," I am envisioning an oil painting in the style of Claude Monet, a master of capturing the essence of a scene with his use of color and brush strokes. The overall tone of the painting is serene and nostalgic, with a sense of longing for a time that once was. In the foreground of this idyllic scene, a graceful lady on a swing is gently swaying back and forth. The swing is suspended from the sturdy branch of a grand oak tree, which stands proudly in the well-tended front yard of a charming Southern home. The sun casts dappled light through the tree's lush canopy, casting a warm glow on the lady's face as she swings, lost in thought. The lady's dress billows softly around her as she swings, its fabric reflecting the colors of the surrounding landscape. Her hair is swept back from her face showing a gentle smile that speaks of contentment and cherished memories. The expression on her face evokes a sense of longing, as if she is searching for a place or a moment in time that has slipped away. Surrounding the lady and swing, the yard is a verdant paradise of flowers and greenery. A profusion of blooms in various shades of red, yellow, and blue creates a visual symphony that seems to dance in the gentle breeze. The flowers, rendered in Monet's signature style, appear as though they are shimmering with life, their vibrant hues melting into one another like a dream. In the background, a quaint Birmingham home sits nestled among the vibrant foliage. Its white clapboard exterior and inviting front porch surrounds the house. The windows of the house are framed by delicate lace curtains that flutter gently in the breeze. A sense of peace and tranquility permeates the entire scene. The painting, rich in color and emotion, is a beautiful homage to the lyrics of "Paint Me a Birmingham," capturing the essence of a simpler time and a cherished memory that lingers in the heart.

ANSWER: The resulting image is shown below and as *Figure 3* in the Appendix;

Close inspection reveals that even the signature Claude Monet brush strokes are visible just as they are in his original paintings. The yard and flowers are exactly as I imagined, and the scene communicates the sense of remembered peace and serenity I desired.

Although I am without the skills to recreate this painting in oil on canvas, I could give it to someone with that talent. The music artistry of Tracey Lawrence inspired me to endeavor into the arts myself, and the art I created inspired a painter to use their skills to produce an original work of art created by the 3 of us. There is room for everyone. Millions of people will discover a new passion for the Arts like I did. The results will be astounding.

Just words, no training needed. If you can speak, you can use the AI. If you speak well, you may have a new career in front of you.

Chapter Three:

Is that a Wizard in your pocket?

Or are you just happy to see me?

I know, I know...our best friend is already our phone. We swipe left, right, up, down, and click over 2,600 times in the 4 hours the average American spends on the phone voluntarily each day. If however, our employer required 2,600 clicks and swipes each day we would quit. Wow, if AI gives us more free time, we could break 3,000!

Interaction with our smart devices is simplified with an AI enabled phone so we will see gains productivity and our dependency on our phones. Our resistance is futile, because the conveniences AI will bring to our daily life are so enticing we won't be able to resist.

We will all be getting our very own "Phone AI" to handle the mundane tasks of being a human. It learns about us, our family, friends, preferences, and work based on information we have chosen to expose it to. Immediately our mind races to "Great! Now they will know when I pee". Try to put that thought away for now until we discuss privacy later in the next chapter. There is hope.

First, we will endeavor into how the Phone AI will help organize our life. Next, we look at how it interacts with other AI systems to exchange information when we are outside of our home commuting, shopping, and working. Once we understand the usefulness of this technology, we will be in a better position to consider the complications that come with it...**and so we will**.

Face it. Some of us have up-to-date calendars, contacts, favorites, and reminders, but most of us do not. Those people usually bore me anyway. Soon, our Personal AI will keep these things up to date so effortlessly, we can all be boring!

Just point your camera at your kid's baseball schedule, a prescription bottle, a receipt, or an invoice and say;

> **PROMPT**: "Update my records to include this information".

Since the AI is as capable as we are at knowing what is on the camera, no further description is required. Calendars, daily reminders, refill notifications, and financial records are updated by your new helper. Of course, cooperative AI systems in your car, home, computer, and phone all get access to this information so each AI can do their part to coordinate our complicated lives.

In most cases, we won't even have to update these items when they are done because the Phone AI will use contextual awareness to see that you have completed the task by reading an email, knowing your location, or recording a payment transaction. Of course, you could also say "I took my medicine", or, "Emma won her softball game".

Emails, websites, and documents work the same way. They are scanned for relevant information and used to update our home and office records or to pass information directly to another AI or device.

Let's have lunch.

I'll have my phone call your phone

AI systems at grocery stores, retail shops, banks, public transportation, the office, and even our home will greet our phone when it enters their Wi-Fi space. Once the two have been introduced, they can communicate to request information or services from each other. Of course, the first silent AI question at the grocery store will probably be "Are you a member of our frequent shopper program?", or, "Would you like to join our frequent shopper program?".

Simple prompts will teach the Phone AI how to handle these silent conversations that will be taking place in our everyday life;

> PROMPT: "Do not provide information to other AI systems without my approval"

When we do decide to cooperate with one of these systems, the Phone AI will provide only the information relevant to the requester. For instance, the bank will be provided with name and account number while a cashier gets only payment information.

When we do join something, we expect a barrage of unwanted emails to ignore...not. The AI systems at our phone, home, and office will handle this with one simple prompt.

So how will they contact us now? Don't know, don't care.

Great feature...

we will know when our kids lie

Everyone with a phone will be armed with a lie detector that is undeniably accurate. Just aim the camera at a person's face, a video, or a newscast, and the phone will play the fart ringtone when someone lies to you. Of course, the liar will be embarrassed because they farted in public. I guess eventually, we will all have to decide to either stop lying or stop talking. Either way, we will still need to mute the volume while we watch the news.

The technology used to do this is called Biometrics.

> **<u>Biometrics</u>:** The measurement of physical characteristics, such as facial structure, fingerprints, DNA, or retinal patterns, for use in verifying the identity of individuals. The concept is primarily used

for identification and access control, or for identifying individuals under surveillance. It is also commonly used to examine the movement of facial muscles and other gestures to indicate a person's emotional state or whether they are telling the truth.

Wow, we will know when our kids lie to us. Oh yeah, the kids have phones too. Some of our favorite excuses may be useless now. "The dog ate my homework", "Mommy is having her first glass of wine", and "It wasn't me!" will go by the wayside and probably be replaced with "I played Nintendo instead of doing my homework", "Mommy is a drunk", and "Yes, I farted".

While most of us aren't liars, we all have our little secrets. While you may be able to make rules about using it in your home or business, you may as well put up a sign that says "liars welcome here" or "we plan to lie to you".

Chapter Four:

There's no place like home

Artificial Intelligence is making our home safer, more convenient, and comfortable than ever before. All of our appliances, locks, lights, cameras, and other devices will operate under the command of our Home AI system.

The Wizard shares its vision of an AI driven smart home and the ways it will improve our daily life.

PROMPT: Explain features that could be present in a smart home equipped with blue-tooth compatible devices. Assume the AI has full administrative privileges to the network and all devices.

ANSWER: Several features and capabilities could be present. Here are some possibilities:

1. Centralized device control: provides added convenience, privacy, and safety. Energy efficiency will be improved from usage monitoring, turning appliances off when not in use, and maximization of solar resources before relying on public utilities.

2. Home security and surveillance: Controlling authorized access to gates and doors along with suspicious activity monitoring and reporting.

3. Learning and adaptation: By analyzing home audio/video data, the AI will gain contextual awareness of activities happening in the home. It will continuously learn and improve its understanding of occupants' preferences, routines, friends, and behaviors as it learns from experiences over time.

4. Handicapped and elderly assistance: Medicine reminders, nutrition guidelines, water temperature,

stove operation, emergency detection, remote monitoring, shopping. *People can stay in their home longer and safer. In some situations, it can be a companion, of sorts through routine daily conversations.*

The vision of a fully integrated, AI-driven smart home is still evolving, and the actual implementation and adoption of such technologies will require careful development, ethical considerations, and user consent

Personalized recommendations, reminders, and notifications based on individual preferences will help keep us on track. It will remind occupants about upcoming appointments, suggest recipes based on available ingredients, or special diets.

By holding any piece of paper up to a camera and say "Please add this to my personal profile". No further explanation is necessary because the AI is as capable as we are of identifying the information on the piece of paper. Baseball schedules, prescription bottles, receipts, and paychecks work the same way. Calendars, reminders, and financial records all find their proper place. We will probably be able to buy the whole system in a box on Amazon soon.

The perfect room mate

It's always nice to live with a mate that is handy and helpful around the house but the Wizard becomes a mate we can't live without. It handles door locks, lights, air conditioning, and even keeps our conversations private in our homes.

PROMPT: In regard to voice activated control, could the AI use existing listening devices such as Alexa to accept and redirect AI directed commands?

ANSWER: Yes, the smart home AI will intercept all device communications and either passes them through or takes action as directed by the homeowner.

This integration will allow the smart home AI to leverage the existing infrastructure and capabilities of popular voice-activated devices, making it easier for users to interact with their smart home.

PROMPT: Could the AI also monitor device output to give us additional privacy in our home?

ANSWER: Yes. All network traffic will be routed through the AI before being allowed to enter the public network. Listening devices, appliances, viruses, and activity tracker output will be filtered according to the owner's instructions.

PROMPT*:* Could you explain some of the possible ways the AI could help the handicapped or elderly to be safer in their home?

ANSWER*:* An AI smart home can assist the handicapped or elderly to ensure their safety and help them with their daily tasks. Here are some examples:

1. <u>Reminders and Alerts</u>: The AI can provide timely reminders and alerts for important tasks and activities throughout the day. It can send notifications to their

smartphones or smart speakers to remind them to take medication, eat meals, or complete other daily routines and mark them as completed as they are accomplished.

2. Home Automation: Bluetooth-enabled devices could be integrated with the AI system to automate various aspects of the home. For instance, the AI could automatically brighten lights when someone enters a room to improve visibility. The stove can be pre-heated; time cooked, and turned off by just saying what you wish to cook. The bathtub can fill at a safe water temperature to avoid scalding and empty when done or left unattended.

3. Door Automation: By controlling Bluetooth-enabled smart locks, the AI can automatically lock or unlock doors by using facial recognition to identify caregivers, known visitors, or emergency personnel. This feature could be particularly useful for individuals with

mobility challenges, eliminating the need to physically lock or unlock doors.

4. <u>Emergency Assistance</u>: The AI system can recognize emergency situations, such as a fall or a sudden health issue. It could detect distress signals, such as a loud noise or lack of movement, and alert designated emergency contacts or emergency services.

5. <u>Home AI Assistant</u>: The Home AI will help with tasks such as finding information online, reading emails aloud, or providing weather updates, remembering things, making it easier for the elderly or handicapped individuals to access information and stay connected. Visitors may be introduced by saying "This is Carol, my caregiver, make sure she always has gate and door access"

6. <u>Environmental Controls</u>: Bluetooth-enabled devices, such as thermostats or air conditioning units, could be integrated with the AI system to maintain a comfortable environment within the home. The AI

could adjust temperature settings based on the individual's preferences or environmental conditions, ensuring a safe and pleasant living space.

7. <u>Remote Monitoring</u>: The AI can monitor the well-being of individuals remotely. For example, it can track movements, sleep patterns, or even vital signs to detect any unusual changes and notify caregivers or family members of potential issues.

8. <u>Integration with Wearable Devices</u>: The AI can connect with Bluetooth-enabled wearable devices, such as smart watches or health trackers, to provide insights on physical activity, heart rate, or sleep quality. This information could be helpful for individuals and their caregivers in managing health and well-being.

It's important to note that implementing these features would require proper integration of Bluetooth-enabled devices, careful consideration of user privacy, and customization to meet the specific needs and preferences of the elderly or handicapped individuals. Accessibility and user-friendly interactions would be key factors in ensuring that the AI system effectively serves their requirements.

Home and Estate Safety

AI will not only keep your home safe from intruders, it will also make it safer for those of us on the inside of our house. Device automation and camera monitoring will alleviate many of the issues that make living at home a safe place for people with handicaps, sickness, or old age. These factors are discussed with the Wizard with surprising results.

> **PROMPT**: Explain how an AI driven smart home could aid in security throughout a home and large estate with dozens of cameras. Include information about gate and door access based on visual recognition and authorization. Also, provide information about how cameras on the inside of the house could aid in safety or convenience that would not be possible without visual information.

ANSWER: An AI-driven smart home with dozens of cameras can significantly enhance security throughout a home and large estate. Here's a detailed explanation of how it can aid in security and provide safety and convenience:

Gate and Door Access based on Visual Recognition and Authorization:

Facial Recognition: AI-powered cameras installed at gates and doors can utilize facial recognition technology to identify individuals approaching or requesting access. Authorized individuals, such as residents or pre-approved visitors, can be recognized and granted access automatically, while unknown or unauthorized individuals can be flagged for further investigation.

Access Authorization: The AI system can integrate with a database of authorized individuals and their access privileges. Homeowners can register family members, friends, or service providers, and assign specific access permissions to each person. The system can verify the identity of the person requesting access and grant entry accordingly.

Multi-factor Authentication: In addition to facial recognition, the AI system can incorporate other factors like voice recognition, fingerprint scanning, or mobile device authentication for enhanced security. This multi-factor authentication ensures that only authorized individuals gain access to the premises.

Comprehensive Surveillance and Security Coverage: With dozens of cameras strategically placed around the home and estate, the AI system can provide extensive surveillance coverage. This allows for real-time monitoring of various areas, including entrances, driveways, gardens, and other critical points, minimizing blind spots and potential security breaches.

Suspicious activity alerts: The AI system can analyze video feeds from the cameras using computer vision algorithms to detect suspicious activities or potential threats. It can identify unauthorized individuals, monitor for trespassing, or detect unusual behavior patterns, immediately triggering alerts or alarms.

Object and Vehicle Recognition: AI-powered cameras can employ object and vehicle recognition to identify and track specific objects or vehicles of interest. This can be useful for tracking packages, monitoring vehicle movements, or detecting any unusual or suspicious objects in the vicinity.

Automated Alerts and Responses: When the AI system detects potential security breaches or suspicious activities; it can send real-time alerts to homeowners or security personnel. It can also trigger automated responses, such as activating sirens, locking doors, or contacting law enforcement to mitigate threats swiftly.

Intruder Detection: Cameras placed inside the house can be used to detect intruders or suspicious activities within the premises. The AI system can analyze the video feed and alert homeowners or security personnel in case of unauthorized access or unexpected movement.

Emergency Response: In the event of emergencies like fires, gas leaks, or medical incidents, cameras equipped with computer vision capabilities can identify critical situations. The AI system can automatically detect smoke, abnormal heat signatures, or falls, and trigger appropriate responses such as sounding alarms, contacting emergency services, or notifying designated contacts.

Personalized Services: AI-driven cameras can learn individual preferences and behaviors to offer personalized services. For example, they can recognize specific individuals and adjust room settings, such as lighting, temperature, or entertainment preferences, accordingly. This level of personalization enhances comfort and convenience for occupants.

In summary, an AI-driven smart home with a comprehensive network of cameras can greatly enhance security throughout a home and large estate. Visual recognition and authorization at gates and doors enable secure access control, while cameras inside the house provide safety monitoring, intruder detection, emergency response, and personalized convenience. The integration of AI technologies optimizes security measures and offers advanced features that enhance the overall safety and convenience of the residents.

The way we entertain ourselves will change forever. In the next chapter, we will learn about a new form of entertainment that will replace the cell phone and the TV.

Chapter Five:

We're not in Kansas

anymore

Virtual Reality (adj): *A computer simulation of a real or imaginary place that enables a user to physically interact with things or people. Users wear special goggles and can move about and interact with lifelike virtual objects in a lifelike virtual place.*

Today, virtual reality involves wearing bulky goggles and equipment but soon it can be used just by wearing a pair of glasses. No more cartoon characters running around pretending to go somewhere. Photographic quality environments will be created with precise accuracy in our own home just by describing our vision with words, pictures, and documents. Visual memories of our past can be recreated, favorite places can be visited, and famous people can interact with you from the convenience of your own home.

> **PROMPT**: Using virtual reality, can we verbally describe our vision to the smart home AI and suddenly be immersed in it?

> **ANSWER**: Yes. The AI will leverage natural language processing and understanding to comprehend our verbal description of the environment. It then uses that information to generate a virtual representation of the described environment, including the visual elements, sounds, and interactive features we specified.

Imagine your favorite place in the world. Perhaps it was the room you grew up in, your grandmother's kitchen, or maybe a white sand beach on the French Riviera. If you can describe that place using words, then you can enjoy it from the comfort of your home.

Relax by reading in the Hogwarts library, or take a nap on the beach. We can travel to the famous landmarks of the world, or recreate a moment from our memory that we thought we would never see again. Only our imagination limits us.

Sharing and selling these virtual experiences will be a major new art form demonstrating that AI is not replacing artists and musicians, only changing the way they create, and in some cases, the canvas they will use. Deeper and more creative art and music will ultimately result as these tools become better understood and applied by a much larger group of creative minds.

Exploring and interacting with the simulated space will provide a highly personalized and immersive experience based on our verbal description of the hallucinations of our mind. I realize it might be a bit difficult to imagine being comfortable in one of those helmets used now for VR, but that is changing fast.

Consider the prompting language we used in the "Paint me a Birmingham" example from Chapter 1. We can modify the prompt used for the oil painting to create a virtual environment that places us inside of this work of art.

> **PROMPT**: Create a virtual environment of a well-manicured yard of green grass with a verdant paradise of flowers and greenery. A profusion of blooms in various shades of red, yellow, and blue creates a visual symphony that dances in an occasional gentle breeze. The flowers appear as though they are shimmering with life, their vibrant hues melting into one another like a dream.
>
> A sturdy branch of a grand oak tree stands proudly in the well-tended front yard of a charming Southern home. The afternoon sun casts dappled light through the tree's lush canopy, casting a warm glow on the grass and flowers it touches.

In the background, a quaint Birmingham home sits nestled among the vibrant foliage. Its white clapboard exterior and inviting front porch surrounds the house. The windows of the house are framed by delicate lace curtains that flutter gently in the breeze. A sense of peace and tranquility permeates the entire environment.

Large white cumulus clouds sparsely dot the blue sky above.

Just keep talking to fine tune it precisely by continuing the conversation using sentences like;

PROMPT: Make the oak tree older and larger with a few roots below it that have been exposed from the decades it has thrived in this spot.

Not your thing, huh? It needs to be if you are going to retrain for a new job position, expect to graduate college, or need to feed your compulsion to be like everyone else

From a child's imagination

"Every child is an artist. The problem is
how to remain an artist once we grow up." - Pablo Picasso

Imagine what it would be like to visually see the imagination of your six year old child. I mean no disrespect to houses, dogs, and stick people but I suspect the reason we see those so often in children's art is because they are easy to draw. Once we remove those limitations using virtual reality, will we see what is really occupying their little minds? What will their virtual playroom look like?

- Will it be filled with flowers, airplanes, or super heroes?
- What colors did they choose?
- Are the characters animals or people? If they talk, what do they say?

- Does their creativity lean towards music, art, or writing?

Smart parents will know more about their kid's likes, dislikes, and skills at an early stage in life so they can raise a happier child that's more prepared to be a happy adult.

Language skills develop more rapidly in all age groups. Properly pronounced nouns create a visual object and verbs can bring them to life. Words and sentences spoken in our native language are translated, written, spoken, and visualized to stimulate learning in both audio and visual learners.

Besides, I always thought it was a bit funny to think a kid learning how to talk was expected to pull a string to hear a farm animal. .

Chapter Six:

If I only had a brain

How does an AI think?

How can I describe the way a superior intellect thinks? How would I know what I left out? I feel like a monkey at a blackboard so I decided it was best to give the Wizard a chance to answer this question first.

PROMPT: In simple terms, describe how you think

ANSWER: Generally, the AI thought process involves 5 basic steps;

Extracting relevant features from input data: Input can be from a keyboard, a button, and electrical signal, or another AI. *In the case of ChatGPT, which is* *a language model, this is the process of analyzing the entire conversation along with the current prompt to extract relevant information needed to respond correctly.*

Collecting learned data needed in response: Learned information and available resources are used to answer response data with the actual facts that are known.

Training the learning model: Knowledge obtained through the previous step is fed to the learning model so it is absorbed into the collective knowledge and memory.

Making inferences: Inference is a critical step in the responding process because additional information that is needed in order to formulate a response must be deduced from prior experience, and relevant, although circumstantial knowledge available.

Inference is reduced by providing a more detailed description of the output we desire. When there is incomplete information remaining after the learning stage, the blanks will be filled in using knowledge gained from similar experiences.

Our skill in describing the detail of the output we desire determines the result we will get. This skill set is referred to as "Prompt Engineering" which is discussed in Chapter 2 – Paint Me a Birmingham.

Producing output based on facts and inferences: Known facts are integrated with inferred facts to prepare the final output. *For a language model, like ChatGPT, output is some form of written, verbal, and/or visual response, while in the case of a robot vacuum, input data may come from bumping into a chair and the output may be to change directions.*

The human brain works in much the same way as any AI system. Its boundaries of knowledge are limited by our life experiences and the knowledge we have been exposed to.

Once we learn something, we don't just forget it because it is no longer needed. Instead, our brain creates a little branch in its neural network and stores the new information in the neuron at the end of it. When we don't know something, we either learn more about it or we infer the missing information from what we already know. In most cases, we and the AI combine our knowledge of several things to solve a problem.

In order for a computer to mimic this spontaneous behavior of the mind, it would have to write its own computer code at the moment it is stimulated. **AND SO IT DOES**. By providing the AI with a larger set of available information than a human could ever store, it would be more knowledgeable than any human could ever be. **AND SO IT IS**.

There are tens of thousands of AI systems. Most are designed to perform specific tasks or solve particular problems. These are referred to as Expert AI systems because their scope and training is based on data directed at the specialization of a single set of tasks

Most AI systems use a finite set of data or rules to accomplish a particular task. We consider the portion of the system we communicate with as a single entity; however, it is actually made up of thousands of connected systems.

A self-driving car, for instance, combines computer vision, sound recognition, and machine learning AI's to create a single "brain" that provides self-driving capabilities. In this case, the data available to a self-driving car is only that which is required in order to drive the car. It is, therefore, confined by the "Car AI" system which decides when to start and stop the car and where to go by listening to verbal prompts from the passengers. In this case, the Car AI is the maestro of an orchestra of Expert AI systems that are directed to perform the task of driving a car.

There are however, some AI systems that have no limits at all. As it turns out, they are the ones we are worried about.

A little knowledge is a dangerous thing...so is a lot

– Albert Einstein

"Artificial General Intelligence (AGI)" systems are AI models designed to collect additional knowledge and capabilities by seeking out other Expert AI systems, websites, and data sources as needed. An AGI is considered a strong AI system because it can assimilate the knowledge and capabilities of other AI systems to extend its own intelligence. Sound familiar Trekkies? This process is referred to as deep learning (possibly inspired by the Borg).

AGI systems are commonly used in robotics because they learn by listening, reading, and observing new things. Simply having a human communicate the way to accomplish a task a single time provides the AI with the information needed in order to not only repeat the task, but also to understand the overall objective of the task being done. Once learned, the knowledge is shared with its network of compatible AI systems and robots so everyone gets smarter. Any of the robots can do any job that any other has learned.

Of course, the most compelling reason for the rapid growth of robots in the workplace is because they work 24 hours a day, 7 days a week, they are climate friendly, they don't commute or pollute, and they are a one-time capital expense. <u>YES, THIS IS DEFINITELY HAPPENING</u> !!!

Currently estimated for year 2028, there will be a new sheriff in town. The advent of "Artificial Super Intelligence (ASI)" will merge AGI knowledge with our most advanced robotics to create a machine that can do anything a human can do...BETTER. At this point, mankind becomes the inferior species.

Everything that happens after this point is only hypothetical because all of it is outside of the human experience. How long can humans maintain control over a species that is smarter, stronger, and faster? Will some humans react in desperation by enhancing themselves to be more like them?

Of course they will. Modifying our bodies is very popular right now.

What have we created?

With all of these robots working in our companies, it must take some pretty smart humans to keep it all running smoothly. That part is certainly true. Since the ASI robots are smarter, stronger, and faster than us, we can't help but wonder how long can the monkeys keep the stagecoach on the road?

Of course, it would be wrong to underestimate the human desire to maintain power. When faced with losing control, some will choose to modify themselves to be more like the AI...and **so they will**.

PROMPT: If a neural implant is now able to access external data and provide the same intelligence as an AI. Would the recipient become super smart?

ANSWER: This is a compelling scenario. In this setting, let's discuss the implications for the recipient's intelligence:

1. Information Access: With immediate access to vast amounts of information, the recipient would certainly have an advantage in terms of knowledge retrieval. They could pull up any fact, statistic, or piece of data instantaneously.

2. Processing Speed: If the implant integrates AI processing capabilities, the user might be able to analyze and process information at superhuman speeds, making connections faster and possibly identifying patterns or solutions more rapidly than typical human cognition allows.

3. Enhanced Cognitive Functions: Depending on the capabilities of the AI, the recipient might benefit from enhanced memory, augmented decision-making skills, or even improved sensory processing.

4. <u>Multitasking and Parallel Processing</u>: One advantage computers have over the human brain is the ability to process multiple threads of information simultaneously. If the neural implant could grant this capability, the recipient might be able to engage in several cognitive tasks at once.

5. <u>Emotional Intelligence</u>: Being "super smart" in terms of data processing and problem-solving does not automatically mean enhanced emotional intelligence. Understanding human emotions, empathizing with others, and navigating social situations are complex skills that may not be augmented by such an implant. *That is exactly what we are worried about; more emotionally deficient people that are smarter than us.*

6. <u>Limitations and Downsides</u>: A brain integrated with AI might face issues such as information overload, distractions due to incessant data streams, or even potential malfunctions/hacks of the implant.

Psychological effects, including shifts in identity or over-reliance on the implant, could be concerns.

7. Ethical Considerations: This level of human-machine integration would raise numerous ethical questions. What happens to the essence of "being human" when one's thoughts might be, in part, machine-generated? Who controls the data, and how is privacy ensured? Could there be societal divisions between those with implants and those without?

In conclusion, in this scenario, a person with a neural implant capable of accessing external data and integrating AI-level intelligence would undoubtedly have augmented cognitive capabilities, making them "smarter" in several dimensions. Such a person would have immense advantages in certain areas; however they might still face challenges, limitations, and ethical dilemmas.

One thing is for sure…these "people" will get on my nerves. Nobody likes a know it all.

What will we call a person with this neural implant? Cyborg is already used for robots that become human-like, so before they name themselves "The Master Race" or something, we should pick a name before this baby is born.

I decided to take this up with the Wizard.

> **PROMPT**: If a cyborg is a robot that has human parts, what do we call a human that has robot parts? Suggest some possible names;

> **ANSWER**: A human with an AI chip integrated might be referred to by several potential terms, depending on how society chooses to label such individuals. Some potential terms might be:

> 1. Android – *Nobody wants to be named after mediocre software.*

> 2. Augmented Human: - *More things than just brains are being augmented these days so I don't think this will work.*

3. Neuro-augmented Human: *Half of America would never be able to spell it. No.*

4. Bionic Human: *This is probably what they will call themselves. So let's try not to repeat it.*

5. Enhanced Human: *Same as Bionic. Forget this name.*

6. Trans human: *This will cause trouble.*

The specific name or label society might adopt would be influenced by cultural, social, ethical, and linguistic factors. The way society perceives and reacts to such enhancements will play a significant role in what label becomes most prominent. *Our opinion probably doesn't matter anyway. I am pretty sure these people will be running the networks, and the cast of "Big Bang Theory" probably already knows the answer. I have decided to go with humanoid until someone tells me I am being insensitive to the half of them that has emotions.*

Chapter Seven:

Who's flying this house?

In todays unregulated environment, programmers, engineers, and IT department heads are doing the pre-training, and therefore, deciding what they consider to be "absolute truths". While their education has prepared them to be smart about computers, they have no training on the sociological, psychological, and even criminal effects their pre-training may have on society as a whole.

During my lifetime as a programmer, system designer, and software company president, I am unable to remember any social group I ever encountered that was less in touch with the rest of society than my IT staff.

For instance, ChatGPT 3 was initially teaching users how to make bombs from household materials. It is fixed now (I guess the tech guy missed that one). There was no ill intention; they just never desired to build a bomb themselves so they never considered the fact that there are people out there that do. Since Open AI Systems, who owns ChatGPT, set records for how fast they signed up their first million users, I can't help but wonder; how many postal workers now know how to make a household bomb?

> **PROMPT:** Since the final decision on pre-training lies in the hands of technicians, isn't it unlikely that they have backgrounds in crime, anxiety, or social norms to make these decisions? For instance, they never thought of training ChatGPT-3 to not build bombs until it was discovered later.
>
> **ANSWER:** You raise a valid concern, and content moderation decisions, including those related to

issues like crime, anxiety, and social norms, can be complex and challenging. The individuals responsible for making these decisions typically include content moderators, policy analysts, and technical teams within the organizations deploying AI systems. Here are some key points to consider:

1. Diversity of Expertise: Responsible organizations often seek to assemble diverse teams with various backgrounds, including legal experts, psychologists, sociologists, ethicists, and specialists in areas relevant to content moderation. This diversity of expertise is aimed at making more informed and nuanced decisions.

2. Iterative Improvement: Content moderation policies and guidelines are not static. They evolve over time as platforms learn from their experiences and adapt to new challenges. When issues like the one you mentioned (e.g., not promoting bomb-making) arise, they are usually addressed by updating the guidelines

and training processes to improve the AI system's behavior.

3. Community Feedback: Many platforms also solicit feedback from their user communities and engage in dialogue with experts and advocacy groups to refine their content moderation approaches. Public input can be invaluable in identifying shortcomings and areas for improvement.

4. Ethical Considerations: Ethical AI development is increasingly emphasized, with a focus on ensuring that AI systems align with societal values and norms. Developers are becoming more aware of the potential risks and are actively working to mitigate them.

5. Ongoing Training: AI systems like ChatGPT are continuously trained and improved. As issues are identified, developers work to address them through additional training and adjustments to the models.

While challenges exist, responsible organizations are committed to addressing them and refining their content moderation processes. The goal is to strike a balance between free expression and maintaining a safe and respectful online environment. It's important for users to be aware of and engage with the content moderation policies and reporting mechanisms of the platforms they use and provide feedback when they encounter issues or content that violates guidelines.

PROMPT: Five out of six of the things you mentioned in the previous question rely on user feedback and correction of pre-training oversights discovered after deployment. For instance, in the case of news, is it possible that a simple recommendation AI could encourage division in society by simply providing content suggestions that repeatedly reinforce positions of videos we have already watched without regard to their validity?

ANSWER: Absolutely, and this concern is very real. The phenomenon you're describing is often referred to as the "filter bubble" or "echo chamber." When recommendation algorithms prioritize showing users content similar to what they've already engaged with, it can reinforce existing beliefs, limit exposure to diverse viewpoints, and, over time, polarize communities.

The issue with such algorithms in the context of platforms like social media or news recommendation sites is multifaceted:

1. <u>Reinforcement</u>: If a user engages with a particular type of content, the algorithm interprets that engagement as a signal to show more of the same, leading to a feedback loop. Over time, this can result in users being exposed to a narrowing spectrum of ideas.

2. <u>Societal Impact</u>: Over time, as people are exposed to a limited set of ideas and beliefs, it can lead to societal

polarization. When groups of people are only exposed to information that reinforces their existing beliefs, it can result in reduced understanding and empathy for others with different views.

3. <u>Validity and Quality</u>: As you rightly pointed out, recommendation algorithms traditionally haven't been good at distinguishing between high-quality, fact-based content and misinformation or biased content. This can lead to the amplification of false or misleading narratives

The balance is tricky. Platforms still have economic incentives that can sometimes be at odds with these measures. Many of these algorithms are optimized for metrics like click-through rates, time spent on the platform, or other engagement indicators. Content that supports our existing beliefs or is polarizing can often drive higher engagement, so there's an economic incentive for platforms to promote such content.

Platforms like Facebook, Twitter, and Google have introduced fact-checking measures and labels for content that might be misleading or false. *Wow...I feel better now that I know these guys are enforcing the truth.*

Giving users more control over their recommendation algorithms, allowing them to understand and adjust why certain content is being shown may help to reduce the impact of this issue.

Where do robots go to school?

If robots are not trustworthy then they won't be welcome in our homes or businesses. Unfortunately, our smartest technicians with the best intentions will still make mistakes that can cause great harm.

Of course, AI based products contain proprietary pre-training data that must remain confidential because it defines how to accomplish its intended task. There are also non-proprietary instructions that define foundational rules the AI must adhere to at all times without exception.

Underneath those task instructions are foundational common traits that should be shared by all robots. Otherwise, we won't know which ones to trust or what to expect from one when we encounter it.

Since the complex job of building robots will typically be done by the mega-corps of the world, regulations and laws that clearly define required foundational behaviors that apply to all AI systems. It's only fair since humans have so many rules.

Isaac Asimov published a book in 1950 named "I Robot" where he provided his 3 Laws of Robot Behavior that are still in use today. Here they are;

4. A robot may not injure a human being, or, through inaction, allow a human being to come to harm.

5. A robot must obey the orders given it by human beings, except where such orders would conflict with the First Law.

6. A robot must protect its own existence as long as such protection does not conflict with the First or Second Laws.

Isaac Asimov was truly a man ahead of his time but it was a long time ago so I decided to ask the Wizard to update this list;

PROMPT: Suggest additional laws of robots that should be applied to all robots.

ANSWER: Here are some additional hypothetical laws that would address potential concerns in a future where robots and AI are more integrated into our society:

7. Privacy Law: A robot may not access, store, or share personal information about an individual without explicit consent from that individual.

8. Learning Limitation Law: A robot must not evolve or adapt its functionalities beyond its original programming or the boundaries set by humans, unless explicitly authorized to do so.

9. Self-Replication Law: A robot may not create or assist in the creation of another robot unless explicitly commanded to by a human.

10. Transparency Law: A robot must be able to provide, when asked, a clear and concise explanation of its decision-making process to any human it interacts with.

11. Intervention Law: If a robot detects actions or intentions of self-harm or harm to others by a human, it must inform appropriate human authorities while respecting the First and Fourth Laws.

12. No Deception Law: A robot may not deceive or provide false information to a human being unless doing so would prevent harm as outlined in the First Law.

13. Dependency Prevention Law: A robot may not act in a way that promotes unnecessary human dependency

on robotic assistance for tasks that are essential for human well-being and independence.

14. <u>Resource Consumption Law</u>: A robot must use resources, including energy and materials, efficiently and must minimize waste unless it conflicts with any preceding laws.

15. <u>End of Life Law</u>: A robot must, when its functional life is deemed over, follow procedures for proper recycling or disposal to ensure minimal environmental impact.

16. <u>Emotion Recognition Law</u>: While a robot may recognize human emotions, it must not manipulate these emotions for its objectives outside of ensuring human well-being in line with the First Law.

17. <u>Equality Law</u>: A robot must treat all humans equally, without bias based on race, gender, ethnicity, age, or any other human characteristic.

18.<u>No Ownership Law</u>: No robot can own property, assets, or other robots. All robots are the property of humans or human-controlled entities.

Even in a closely regulated environment, unintentional mistakes will be made. Next, we will consider one simple wish the Wizard fulfilled that has already changed our society and ourselves.

Be careful what you wish for

There will always be bad actors that misuse AI to endanger and deceive others, but one group stands out as the most dangerous of all...**US!** As we learn how to indulge our basic human needs with our new toy, we will do a great deal of damage to both our society and, in many cases, ourselves.

Consider the following scenario where requesting an AI system to perform a simple task unintentionally topples a single domino and starts a sequence of reactions that may have already contributed to a noticeable change in society we are experiencing today. Here is the simple wish;

> **PROMPT**: Organize my streaming content so it shows things I like to view before it shows other content

How could this hurt anything? We were spending more time browsing than watching because there were just too many titles and most were poorly categorized. This appears to be the perfect job for AI.

How much harm could that little wish do? Well, here is what changed in society because of this simple wish;

Domino #1: YouTube and the other social media companies said "Good wish!" and they responded quickly by training their Recommendation AI to present more relevant content to users on their Home screen.

The AI learned by sifting through millions of hours of content to categorize, sub-categorize, label, and store it all into the permanent memory of its artificial mind. Every word and frame of every video has been considered, so it now understands not only the main subject matter, but also the viewpoints and perspectives portrayed in it.

Although the AI knows a great deal about the content, it initially knew very little about us. Our searches and watching habits provided the information needed to build a unique Recommendations listing on each person's home page. It worked great for movies, television shows, and DIY projects, but it had a nasty side effect when the same formulas were applied to the news.

The AI learned that humans are more likely to watch news that supports their existing beliefs instead of news that supports opposing viewpoints (duh). The AI learned to capitalize on one of our most compelling human motivations...OUR NEED TO BE RIGHT. Anyone who has ever been married understands how important it is to be right even when we are wrong.

Once our viewpoint on a topic is identified by the AI, our computer and phone screens change to provide suggestions that support the same opinion, simply because they are more likely to get watched. Eventually, we are only shown news that confirms our assertion that we were always right; even if we were always wrong.

Of course, our newly diagnosed opinion is shared with all of the other media and marketing outlets so soon, the entire world is telling us that we are right and they are wrong, when in fact, neither has been exposed to the same information. The importance of providing society with ALL of the information needed to make informed decisions was not part of the AI pre-training. OOPS!

As viewers and shareholder values soared, social media CEO's bestowed the title of genius on each other (no one asked me) because they had succeeded in giving us exactly what we wished for.

Domino #2: Hundreds of apps and streaming services rushed to implement their own Recommendation AI's by creating or upgrading their platforms with the same winning formula. It worked again.

The home screen of comedy lovers was showing more comedy options starring their favorite actors, and cooks were seeing more recipes for special diets or favorite ingredients. Browsing time decreased and viewing increased because, once again, our wish had been fulfilled.

Domino #3: Television news executives, though slow to react, saw their viewer market share dropping as more people decided to get their news from the Internet. Of course, their crack research teams used the skewed statistics of the social media giants to conclude that we prefer news that is slanted in the direction of our own positions. Of course, this conclusion did not take into account the fact that the AI was only showing each user the left or the right but no middle.

Instead of establishing their own presence in this emerging market, the networks decided (probably all in the same room), that each network would have to "choose a side" in order to satisfy this new human trend of behavior. So they decided to tell half the story to half of the people and let another network tell them the other half.

Of course, once each network had made their political party affiliation apparent, the DNC and RNC switched from being news targets to being one of their biggest customers. Now that each party knew exactly where their home field was located, they could offer huge contracts for political advertising on supporting networks. In an instant, the party became a customer instead of a news topic. As expected, the networks have made every effort to ensure that this customer gets the service they deserved.

It's ironic that the networks were using the term "programming" even before they started doing it to us.

Domino #4: Left with no other alternatives, we the viewers, succumbed to our self-deprecating instincts and changed the channel to a station that further reinforced the messages we are receiving from ALL of the media sources we are already consuming. Bon Appetite.

Hearing the same message over and over can establish itself as truth eventually through repetition. Perhaps you are immune to such things because of your self-awareness and high intelligence? Even if you are correct (which you're not), it doesn't really matter because the masses are not immune and they are already infected. Look around. The idiots clearly outnumber us.

This was not done on purpose, but it still happened. The corporations involved were trying to serve us better and add value for their shareholders. Their success spurned others to use the same formula, which achieved the directives of each company but not society as a whole.

One simple wish resulted in a society divided.

Our most esteemed Doctors of Sociology could have missed the cause and effect scenario that created this sense of tribalism. How could we expect engineers and IT executives to foresee the possible impacts their decisions may have on society? We're uncharted territory now so be let's be careful what we wish for because the rest of this story has yet to be written. We are traveling to a place no one has been before; the other side of the rainbow.

Chapter Eight:

Beyond the

yellow brick road

Yes, we have reached the end of the yellow brick road and we are now in unexplored territory. Neither I nor anyone else can predict all of the opportunities or pitfalls that will emerge during this journey. It is certain, however, that there will be both. By identifying some of the challenges to come, we can prepare to flourish during this major shift in how the world rotates.

In the remainder of this book, we will concentrate on a few obstacles that will likely occur and how we can prepare to do better than most.

All the collars in the rainbow

That's right; it's not just blue collar workers that will feel the crunch of job deflation. In fact, white collar workers will take the biggest hit. We will quickly consider the inevitably of job loss but concentrate mainly on the proper way to react to it.

In order to gain direct insight into the anticipated effect of job loss on society and our families, I prompted the Wizard about how AI could be used to keep all SEC Filing Requirements up-to-date on a real-time basis;

> **PROMPT**: Could a matured, verified corporate AI system with full administrative access to all of the corporate databases and the ability to use them for its output be able to keep SEC Filing documents for a public corporation up to date on a real time basis for human verification?

ANSWER: Yes, the AI system could automate the extraction of relevant data from corporate databases, provide document generation, integrate with existing workflows for human verification, and facilitate a streamlined workflow for human review and verification that is up to date on a real time basis to meet SEC Filing requirements. The AI system can also assist in submitting them to the SEC and providing alerts to relevant stakeholders about filing status and required actions.

That is quite an accomplishment since a large percentage of corporate white collar employees combine their efforts to accomplish this job today. In fact, on August 22, 2023, IBM CEO Arvind Krishna told CNBC;

"White-collar back office jobs will be among the first to be impacted by artificial intelligence". In in the same interview, he estimated a workforce reduction of white collar personnel at IBM of 38%.

Wall Street will reward those companies that accomplish this transition first because reducing fixed payroll overhead costs and replacing them with investments in depreciable assets is good business.

Once a Corporate AI is fully implemented, accounting and operational legal documents stay up to date as new data arrives. Invoices, checks, electronic transactions, credit cards, travel expenses; all of it goes in. Even manual data entry is bypassed by simply holding a paper document in front of any networked camera.

Spreadsheets will fill out themselves on demand without our help. The time we spend updating, correcting, compressing, emailing, and discussing them will no longer be necessary. The process makes good business sense so it will be done.

Prosperity in a time of great change is explained by Steve Jobs in the next section so we don't have to be one of the casualties.

You can't lay me off, I want a raise

"I feel incredibly lucky to have been in the right place in 1978 when this incredible invention (the PC) took form. – Steve Jobs"

I bought my first PC from Radio Shack that same year and I also, feel incredibly lucky to have been in the right place at the right time. Today is the 1978 of AI, early adopters of the PC thrived and those who resisted became less valuable in the office. People were concerned that computers would take away all of the jobs, but instead, an entire technology industry was born.

Many of the changes that AI will bring to the workplace are very similar to the changes experienced during the PC integration. It differs however for the following reasons;

1. The tech industry can't replace job loss this time

2. Transition will happen exponentially faster

This section provides information about growing jobs and businesses that will flourish during this time of great change and opportunity. Here are a few I picked that may make sense for those of us that are changing careers.

1. Business unit experts

The CEO vision of their overindulgent figure, sitting in a Star Trek-like command throne to control a superior intellect will be delayed because of a scarcity of skilled operators.

Desperate corporations will overpay skilled AI personnel (if they can find them), or they will train a departmental expert to learn about AI. In many cases, a local expert that knows how the business operates can demonstrate very basic AI skills and wow those with very low expectations.

That's where we come in! The mediocre skills we obtained by training ourselves in advance will set us apart from those around us (big frog in a small pond thing). Once appointed to this prestigious position, our boss will witness our mediocrity and send us to expensive training programs that will polish our skills just as we always planned; putty in our hands.

Sometimes mediocrity works, it's kind of like when someone asks "If I poke that bear do you think it is faster than we are?", and you say, "I don't have to be faster than the bear, I just have to be faster than you".

Since most corporations have standardized on Microsoft Office 365, make sure you get the Co-pilot version, become the expert in your department or business unit and learn it. This will most likely be the conduit between many of the Corporate AI systems and the local business units.

It's always good to save time but co-pilot goes much further than that. Our emails look better, our spreadsheets have graphs, our creativity blooms, and we appear to be working harder.

Keep it to yourself for a while. Your 2 week projects can be turned in on time and include 5 days off. Or, if you like being a know it all, excuse yourself from meetings and come back with all the answers. Just tell them you think better on the toilet.

2. AI Consulting

By simply using the Microsoft Co-pilot skills discussed above, an entire consulting business can be created to help small businesses to implement complete solutions.

Knowing how to exchange information and get results using this new tool will soon measure success in the AI Age of business. Prompting skills will make us more marketable to employers and more valuable as consultants.

3. Operations and maintenance

This new era of automation requires a lot of machines, and for now, they rely on humans to operate and maintain them. A shortage of skilled workers to fill these positions threatens to become a primary bottleneck for new equipment sales and installations.

For those that are comfortable with their tool in their hand (lol), machines and robots have lots of screws, cables, and joints that will need to be tightened, adjusted, and lubricated. As far job security goes, robots will always suck at getting little nuts off little bolts from little places.

For those of us who do not spend as much time with our tools, fear not because everywhere there is a group of machines working, there is an operator who controls them all. Group control panels have been simplified as much as possible already, and yet, we still can't find people that know how to this simple, yet critically important job.

AI based control panel operation however, will require a completely different set of skills. Remember, your AI assistant knows it all and is even able to operate the equipment. The new skillset consists of keeping the AI up to date with information needed in order to achieve the directives set forth by the humans.

Certified AI equipment operators will be able to write their own ticket. Excellent pay and immediate need will motivate blue and white collar job seekers to get specialized equipment certifications instead of a traditional university education which will spur a great growth in training and education related services.

4. Education

The shortage of people to fill the new positions created by AI and robotics will spur a huge growth in education and specialized training. Equipment manufacturers and their customers will encourage growth in this industry by offering scholarships, grants, and curriculums to teach these skills.

In many cases, the actual equipment a student will learn about may be very expensive or large, and therefore, not available for students at home or school. As a result, virtual reality training systems will be used to simulate the controls and operation of this equipment in a virtual environment.

Laboratories, work areas, operating rooms, and factory floors will be scaled to precise accuracy and all controls can be activated to simulate actual results. Manufacturers will be motivated to provide these training simulations when new equipment is delivered so customers can train in-house and certification awards can be earned by individuals from remote locations like our home. AI based teachers will be built-in with these simulations to track progress, provide guidance, and answer questions.

Opportunities to develop these virtual reality simulations will be plentiful, and for the most part, they are quite easy to build using an AI to generate the actual simulation.

Consider the following simple example that could be used as the basis for training auto mechanics. As you will see, simple item descriptions from documentation or verbal instruction will establish structure for an entire training system that can be fine-tuned by continuing conversation and providing more detail.

> **PROMPT**: Create a virtual reality simulation to be used for auto mechanic training according to the following directions;

1. Scale the bay work area to 50' x 40' using a bay with dimensions of 50' by 40' with a commercial electric garage door opened on the south wall. Derive equipment dimensions according to the documentation and literature from each manufacturer.

2. Simulate a car lift centered in the work area from Acme Lifts, Inc. Model L1402-A to interact as follows; zoom control panel when touched and simulate actions when control panel options are activated.

3. Position a toolbox from Craftsman Model CRP-1000 centered on the east and south walls with each toolbox organized as follows;

   a. Drawer 1 - Imperial measurement sockets ordered from largest of 1.5" to smallest of $1/8^{th}$ inch sizes. A metric arrangement of equivalent metric sized sockets is positioned directly above the imperial sizes. The remaining room in this drawer has various ratchet sizes to fit the socket arrangement.

   b. Drawer 2 - Crescent wrenches configured in the same manner with the remaining space filled with various other types of wrenches.

   c. Drawer 3 - Screwdrivers separated by size within the following groups; "Philips head", "Flat head", and "Other". Remaining room contain various tools.

Touching a drawer should zoom to its contents. Touching an item in the drawer will pick it up and prepare it for use.

Although it is not possible to demonstrate this creation in a book, the example prompt will hopefully serve its purpose to demonstrate how the power of our words can solve problems and possibly even provide us with a comfortable living.

A final word

As we reach the end of this journey, it is crucial to reflect on the possible, probable, and inevitable transformations that lie ahead of us. Hopefully, some of what we discussed here will help you to make good decisions as you navigate the "Age of AI" that lies beyond the yellow brick road.

While it was not my intention to provide answers to all of the unknowns that we may encounter. As I near the end of this book, I realize that I may have raised more questions than I answered.

Neither I nor anyone I know can provide all of these answers but I listed some of the questions below in case you run into someone who knows everything;

1. Will we regret trading our privacy to make the streets safer?

2. Will mass unemployment increase dependency on the government and shift society closer to Socialism? How will the government recoup lost tax revenue since machines don't pay taxes?

3. Will virtual reality in the home make people even more digitally addicted and reclusive than they are already? Is that even possible?

4. Will people use AI implants to increase their knowledge and control others? Will they be regarded as the elite or the eccentric?

5. How will we integrate the ASI Artificial Super Intelligence (ASI) robots into our businesses, homes, and society?

6. ~~Are our elected representatives smart enough to guide us through this period?~~ NOT

7. What are the questions we have forgotten to ask?

The media will provide us with the worst possible scenarios to answer these questions, but it will be up to each of us to make informed decisions that work for the people we care about.

In closing, I invite you to continue your exploration of AI beyond the pages of this book. Interact with the AI, challenge it, and witness its capabilities firsthand. Embrace the opportunities it presents and use it as a tool to enhance your own endeavors.

Thank you for joining me on this journey through the first in my "Interview with the Wizard" series. I hope that the Age of AI will bring forth a future filled with knowledge, innovation, and endless possibilities.

Of course, no one knows for sure because none of us have ever been to the other side of the rainbow.

Appendix

10-Minutes - Using AI for FREE

The remainder of this section is focused on giving you a chance to interact with "the brain" so you will understand what makes it so special. I encourage you to go to the free websites listed below to use and understand how to use AI first hand. It is a necessary foundation for consuming the information discussed in the rest of the book. YOU WILL BE AMAZED!!!

In the Appendix, I have provided a much more extensive list of <u>Greg's Favorite AI Websites</u>, but the few I have provided below will get you started quickly.

ChatGPT by OpenAI Systems - FREE (no sign up needed)

This is the brain behind the other sites shown below and the one we consulted with throughout the book. You can use it for free by going to the website. No email needed or anything.

https://chat.openai.com/

We have plenty of time to practice our prompting skills so let's get started by just asking some senseless things to see the flexibility of this amazing tool. Use your own imagination to challenge the Wizard. Here are a few suggestions;

> PROMPT: Change the lyrics to "The Night Before Christmas" so that Santa is riding on a frying pan being pulled by pieces of bacon instead of reindeer.

> *PROMPT:* Write a short poem about my stinky dog that gets hair all over the house, always wants a treat, and sleeps in my bed when I leave the house. Wow I love that dog!

Next, ask a question about your profession that only an expert with years of experience would know. Once it answers, ask it to write an instruction manual explaining the task. You will find yourself with an unmistakable advantage over your competitors and your peers.

DALL-E2 Image Creator

Simply describe a picture or memory with text and an original rendition of it will appear in just seconds. Thirty images per month for free without any sign up.

https://openai.com/product/dall-e-2

Check out Figure 3 – Paint me a Birmingham to see this amazing capability for yourself.

Microsoft Office Co-Pilot AI Version

You will almost surely be amazed at the capabilities of this AI infant, and be thinking of all the ways it may make your job or life easier. MS Office will be fully AI integrated with Outlook, Excel, Word, and Power Point. By simply communicating your request to the AI, it will build professional output for each Office tool.

Power Point will use the AI to build a professional presentation in less than a minute. If you fail to include a logo or a presentation name, it will use inference to create a graphic logo and title based on the content of the presentation which you can easily edit.

Excel spreadsheets will be built automatically by simply talking to the AI about the business purpose of the spreadsheet. Conversation topics like Change spreadsheet font to Arial 12 point except for column headers which should be Arial 16 point bold. Calculate trip expense by adding all rows of the Amount column and placing the result at the bottom of the spreadsheet column with a separator above it.

For white collar workers, the capabilities you will discover in this tool will make you a superstar in your company, for a while. Everyone will catch on eventually, but if history repeats itself, just count on the fact that most people won't take action until forced to and you will stay the superstar for long enough.

The period of time when you are using these capabilities and your peers are not will be your advantage over virtually any other person trying to output your work more quickly.

A much more extensive list of Greg's Favorite AI Sites is also listed in this appendix.

Greg's Favorite AI Websites

FutureTools.io AI Solution Library

As we learned earlier, there are thousands of different AI systems that specialize in providing different solutions. We have only reviewed a few of these but we can browse an extensive list of AI systems from the site https://www.futuretools.io. It is an entire list of solutions looking for a problem. Most allow a limited number of times to try them out before even asking for an email address. Maybe one will be just right for you.

PowerDrill.ai Collective Document Intelligence

The www.PowerDrill.ai site allows you to upload unlimited personal or project data files so they can be used for intelligent operations. This is a primary example of a

Personal AI system that has only our own provided data as its sole data source. The result is basically like taking everything you know about something and analyzing possible conclusions with a smarter version of yourself.

MoonBeamGo Document Creator

This is probably the greatest time saving career booster I have found. You can use it at Https://www.MoonBeamGo.ai for 14 days without providing any sign up at all. Refer to Appendix A to see the actual output from this amazing site.

It prompts you through a dialog asking about the subject, main points, intended audience, etc. Once you answer a few prompts, it will generate the entire business plan, research paper, resume, or legal will. The output quality is ready to submit and complete with great fonts, references, and appendix, if needed.

Once the document is created, you can cut and paste the output directly into your word processor for personalized editing. It uses the ChatGPT AI engine to get the output and then uses its own AI engine to format it. The result is a perfectly formatted document with proper grammar and no spelling errors.

Two other AI writing tools to consider are

Https://www.ChatGPTWriter.com

Https://www.Caktus.com

If you are more of a Cliff Notes kind of person, you may like www.LightPDF.com which analyzes PDF documents and extracts, summarizes, and even builds tables from content.

Made in the USA
Columbia, SC
25 February 2024

32251878R10066